UNEXPLAINED SNIGLETS OF THE UNIVERSE

RICH HALL & FRIENDS

Illustrated by Arnie Ten

ALFRED HITCHCOOKING *(al' fred hich' cooh king)*
v. Continuously stabbing at a block of frozen
vegetables to make them cook faster.

UNEXPLAINED SNIGLETS OF THE UNIVERSE

(snig' lit):
any word that doesn't appear in the dictionary, but should

Collier Books • Macmillan Publishing Company • New York

Collier Macmillan Publishers • London

Macmillan Publishing Company
866 Third Avenue, New York, N.Y. 10022
Collier Macmillan Canada, Inc.

Library of Congress Cataloging-in-Publication Data
Hall, Rich, 1954–
Unexplained sniglets of the universe
1. Words, New—English—Anecdotes, facetiae, satire,
etc.—
2. Vocabulary—Anecdotes, facetiae, satire, etc.
I. Title.
PN6231.W64H34   1986   428.1'0207
85-23179
ISBN 0-02-040400-X (pbk.)

10 9 8 7 6 5 4 3

Designed by Antler & Baldwin, Inc.
PRINTED IN THE UNITED STATES OF AMERICA

To Darby

CONTRIBUTORS

Marc Allen Mel Abveg Jim Bailey Matt Besterman Mike Bivens Connie Boyd Gene Brown Dean Burgess Drew Butler Debbie Cantrell Lynn Carlson Al Causey Keith Cerasoli Andrew Chatterson Derek Clawson John C. Coble Dave Coey Matthew Cordo Donald Cililla Brian Cullinan Steven Cortina Tyler Deans Perry Dennis Stephen Dyer Lynn and Joel Eskin Linda Felten Michael Francisco Joe Garagiola Alex Gastgeb Todd Gerber Lou Gershenson David Gross Jim Grybowski **Rich Hall** Pat Hamlett Mack Hendricks Teresa Holik Tom Huber Geof Huth Eric Johnston Neal Katz John D. Kellog Nick Kosan Jr. Bill Kraft Kris Kranig Don Kinzel Teddy Kruljac Mike Kundak Michael Laird Jack Laurie Chris Leavell Chris Levi Dean Lewis Patrick Leyba Ray and Lisa Daniele Lussier Liz Matheny Ryan Maynes Karen Meyer Tom Mikita Bob Myles Gary Muldoon Ryan Nelson Dave Newman Mike O'Shea Kris Parker Mike Payne David Perazzo Ken Post Shane Poulter Jeff Radoicic Harry Ralston Brian Raslawski Carol Reichiert Paula Reisinger John Rhodes Tony Roberti David Robertson Richard Rosalia Jim Rosen Tom Russell Eric Saphire Ev Schafer Frank Scaldone Tony Scacifero Cindy Seglowich Steve Serra Ira Shain Jonathan Shandell Mike Siggins Jim Sippola Cheryl Six Stephanie Snow Brian Stewart Ross Storm Scott Strent Tim Thomas Matt Thompson Jonathan Tully Florence Tummolo Richard Vickroy John Wiening Mary Weiss Adert Welkin Robert J. Woodhead L. N. Yarbrough Chris Zarcone Vincent Zedler

CONTENTS

UNEXPLAINED SNIGLETS OF THE UNIVERSE

ACELLOYELLOS
(a sel' oh yel' oz)

n. People who speed through caution lights.

AGE OF CLAUSABILITY
(ayj' uv klaw' za bil' ih tee)

n. The point at which we stop believing in Santa.

AIRCAPPED
(ayr' capt)

v. To be temporarily crippled when the airplane passenger in front of you drives his seat back into your knees.

AIRPUNT
(ayr' punt)

n. Any of a series of kicks that advances one's baggage toward the airport counter.

ALFALFABET
(al fal' fuh bet)

n. Backward letters used only on clubhouse doors.

ALFRED HITCHCOOKING
(al' fred hich' cooh king)

v. Continuously stabbing at a block of frozen vegetables to make them cook faster.

ANANANANY
(an a na' na nee)

n. The inability to stop spelling the word "banana" once you've started.

ANAFONDICS
(an a fon' diks)

n. Exercising to a workout album at 16 RPM.

APPLAFLAMMAPHOBIA
(ap la flam uh fo' bee uh)

n. Fear that upon departing for vacation, you've left an appliance on that will burn the house to the ground.

AQUACOUSTICS
(ak wa koo' stiks)

n. Sound waves in the bathroom that enable anyone to sing on key.*

ASPIRBAYERPERPAIR-PERFECTION
(as pur bayr' pur payr' pur fek' shun)

n. The ability to always extract *exactly* two headache tablets from the bottle.

ASTEREXASPER
(as tuhr eggs as' pur)

n. An asterisk with no corresponding footnote.

AULDLANXIETY
(old lang zi' et ee)

n. Experience of waking up on New Year's Day and wondering how much of a fool you made of yourself.

AWSLICE
(aww' slice)

n. The first slice of a wedding cake. The one which ruins the design and causes everyone to sigh.

AZUGOS
(as' you goes)

n. Items to be carried upstairs by the next ascending person.

BARFIUM
(bar' fee um)

n. The horrible smelling cleanser they mop down school corridors with.

BACKIN-MYDAY ACT OF 1901
(bak' in my' day akt uv nein' teen oh wun')

n. Law created in the early part of the twentieth century which made it mandatory to build schools at least 20 miles away from all future grandfathers.

BALLYBUSTER
(bal' lee bus tur)

n. A pinball machine with one dead flipper.

BARBALYSIS
(bar ba' lih sis)

n. Condition that arises from having to keep your head motionless while getting a haircut.

BARCUUMING
(bar' ku ming)

v. Using the family dog to remove the crumbs that have dropped to the floor.

BEVAMIRAGE
(bev' uh mih rahj)

n. Deceiving black ring around the bottom of a two-liter soda bottle.

BLISTERPEG
(blys' tur peg)

n. The irritating part of a thong or flip flop that holds your foot on.

BLOG
(blahg)

n. Overly generous deposits of fish food floating at the top of an aquarium.

BLOSSOR
(blos' er)

n. Unique "winged" hairstyle achieved after wearing a baseball cap for several hours.

BROOP
(broop)

n. The useless pocket on a pajama top.

BURGATORY
(ber' ga tawr ee)

n. The place where unsold burgers go when the stand shuts down for the night.

BUTTRAS
(but' ruhs)

n. Those small buttons in a plastic bag that accompany finer clothing.

CANTWITIONIST
(kan twi' shun ist)

n. Person who manually "rushes" the lid on an electric can opener.

CARPILLARY ACTION
(kar' pih ler ee ak' shun)

n. Property that enables water to move up a windshield when the vehicle is in motion.

CHEDDARBLISTER
(ched' ur blihs tur)

n. The bubble formed when making a grilled cheese sandwich.

CHOCOZIPPER
(chok' oh zip ur)

n. The tab that releases a Hershey's Kiss.

CHOCTASY
(chok' ta see)

n. The joy of discovering a second layer of chocolates underneath the first.

CHRONESIA
(kron ee' zyuh)

n. The tendency not to know the time when asked, even though you've just checked your watch.

CINEDRAFT
(sin' uh draft)

n. The mysterious rush of air that sucks your money into the ticket window at the movie theater.

CINEPLEGIC
(sih neh plee' jik)

n. A person whose foot has temporarily lost circulation from being wedged between theater seats.

CIRCUMVACULATE
(sur kum vak' yew layt)

v. To remain stationary while vacuuming in a circle around oneself.

COINOPHONY
(koy' nah foh nee)

n. Annoying pocket concerts conducted by people who like to jingle keys and change, often accompanied by a rocking motion.

COMEONDOWNS
(kum on downz')

n. Depression resulting from knowing all the answers to a game show while confined in your living room.

CORNISECTION
(kor' nih sek shun)

n. The systematic consumption of candy corn by sections, first biting off the white zone, then the orange zone, then the yellow zone.

3.72 FEET

3.72 INCHES

WRONG

RIGHT

CRAVAMETER
(kra' va mih tur)

n. 3.72 inches, the proper distance between the ends of a tied tie.

CROONO EN FLAGRANTE
(krew' noh on fla grahn' tay)

v. To be caught singing to the muzak when the secretary takes you off hold.

CRUSTADJUSTER
(krus' ta jus tur)

n. The "light-dark" knob on a toaster that makes you think you're in control.

CUBESTACLE
(kewb' stack ul)

n. A person who, no matter where he stands, gets in the way of someone shooting pool.

CUFFLATCH
(kuf' lach)

v. To grasp the edge of one's sleeve to keep it from slithering up the arm while pulling on a sport jacket.

CURDUNDANCY
(kur dun' dan see)

n. The big deal of opening and closing the theater curtains between preview and feature in movie theaters, presumably to help justify the five-dollar admission.

CURODDS
(kur' ohds)

n. The adhesive bandages at the bottom of the box designed for extremely unusual injuries.

DENNIDIOTS
(den id' ee uts)

n. People who actually fill out those "How-was-the-service" exams on the backs of restaurant checks.

DIAGONERD
(dy ag' oh nurd)

n. Person who angles his car across two spaces to keep people from parking too close.

DUDOUT
(dud' owt)

n. Condition of having consumed all of one's snack bar items before the movie even started.

DÜNKEN HÄCKEN
(dun' kin ha' kin)

n. Violent coughing attack brought on by inhaling the powdered sugar on a doughnut.

ECTOLACTO
(ek toh lak' toh)

n. That curtain of milk that runs down the outside of the glass when you try to pour it into the cereal bowl.

EGGORY
(eg' er ee)

n. The part of the fridge that holds the eggs.

ELEMENO
(LMNO)

n. The centermost letter in the alphabet. The one that reduces it from twenty-six characters to twenty-three.

ESSOASSO
(es oh as' oh)

n. A person who cuts through a service station to avoid a red light.

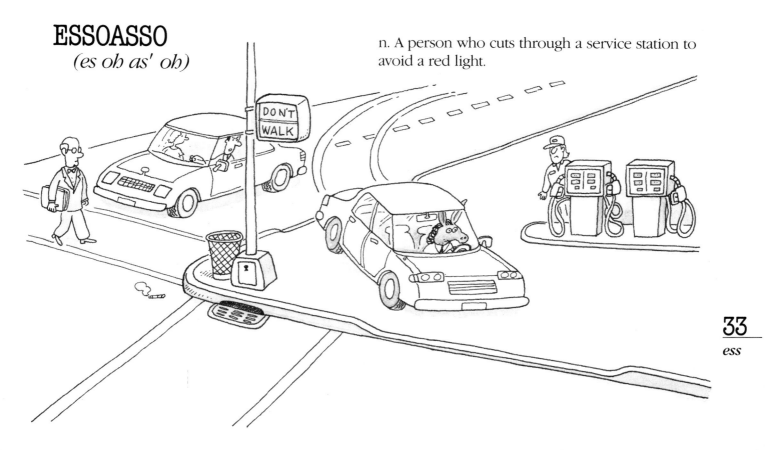

EXCESS BUNNERAGE
(eks' es bun' ur aj)

adj. When the buns at a cookout come in eight packs and the hot dogs in sixes.

EXCESS WIENERAGE
(eks' es wee' nur aj)

adj. When the buns come in eight packs and the hot dogs in twelve. (See also **FRANQUILIZED**.)

EX-O-VAC
(ex' oh vak)

n. The third battery in a "buy two get one free" package that is useless unless you buy a second pack.

FALOOTER
(fa lew' tur)

n. The rope running through a menu that lets you know you're at a fancy restaurant.

FARRELPHOBIA
(fayr el foh' bee yuh)

n. Fear of being approached by several dozen waiters singing, "Happy Birthday."

FEASERS
(fee' zurz)

n. The racing stripes on tennis shoes that fool kids into thinking they can run faster.

FIGFORCE
(fig' fawrs)

n. Mysterious magnetic force that holds two or more Fig Newtons together.

FIRSSUE
(fur' shew)

n. The lead tissue. The one that gets all the others going.

FLEABAGE
(flee' baj)

n. Excess of flea collar that has to be cut off.

FOOMLET
(foom' lit)

n. The bathroom towel you're not allowed to use because it's marked "guest," and guests don't use because who wants to be the first person to mess it up?

FOOPERS
(foo' perz)

n. Passers-by at restaurant windows who stop to watch you eat.

FRANQUILIZED
(frank' wil ized)

adj. When, by some miracle, you have an equal number of buns and wieners at a cookout.

FUTILITY INFIELDER
(few til' ih tee in' feel dur)

n. One who tries to stop grounders by throwing his glove at them.

GARBPACTION
(garb pak' shun)

v. The act of cramming just one more item into a garbage can to avoid emptying it.

GENTREA
(jen' tree uh)

n. The small area of the windshield beneath the steering wheel used by elderly drivers.

GEOUCH
(jee' owch)

n. The sharp rock one always finds directly beneath his sleeping bag.

GREEPERS
(greep' ers)

n. People who walk up the down escalator in an attempt to appear motionless.

GUNKOLEUM
(gun koh' lee yum)

n. The horrible black paste that car manufacturers smear under car seats.

GYMBOLS
(jim' bolz)

n. Those lines and markings on a gym floor that have no purpose whatsoever.

HALASKA
(ha las' kuh)

n. The boxed area on a U.S. map where our 49th and 50th states are located.

HEMOPLUGS
(hee' moh plugz)

n. Small pieces of toilet paper applied to shaving wounds.

HIGHYIMES
(hi' yimes)

n. Those 800 number operators who threaten to return at the end of the magazine subscription commercial to "tell you how to receive your free gift."

HOOPTOOTS
(hoop' tewts)

n. Strange bugle sounds at basketball games, the source of which no one seems to be able to identify.

IDIOLOCATION
(yd' ee oh low kay' shun)

n. The spot on the shopping mall map marked, "you are here."

ILLUMINOT
(il ew' mih naht)

n. Device in airplane bathrooms that won't let the light come on until you lock the door.

IMPASSENGERS
(im pas' enj urz)

n. Two people, one inside the car, one outside, negating each other's actions while trying to unlock the door.

INELVITABLE
(in el' vih tuh bul)

adj. The uncanny ability of a band in old Elvis Presley movies to materialize from nowhere whenever Elvis begins to sing.

INKNITION
(ink nih' shun)

n. The metal clicker at the top of a cheap ball point pen that: a) puts it into operation and b) is also perfect for driving substitute teachers crazy.

INNINGFRINGEMENT
(in ning frinj' ment)

n. The warning near the end of a baseball broadcast that says you better not try to start your own station and "rebroadcast the accounts and descriptions of this game."

JAVAJETSAM
(ja va jet' sum)

n. Washed ashore coffee grounds on the rim of the cup.

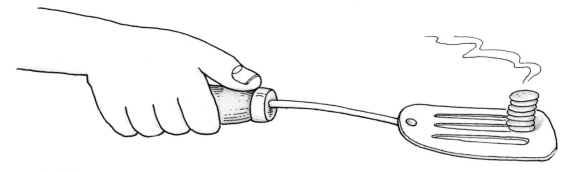

JEMIMITES
(je my' myts)

n. Extremely tiny pancakes formed from the batter that fell off the ladle.

JUJUSPECTION
(joo' joo spek shun)

v. Holding a jujube up to the cinema screen in order to determine its color.

KEYLONIUS
(key loan' ee us)

adj. The slight trace of criminality one feels when having his keys duplicated.

LEXICAVES
(leks' ih kayvz)

n. Indentations on the side of a dictionary.

LEXPLEXED
(leks' plekst)

adj. Unable to find the correct spelling for a word in the dictionary because you don't know how to spell it.

LIGS
(ligz)

n. The two small metal tabs that hold an Ace bandage in place.

LINENARCTICA
(lin en ark' tik uh)

n. The corner of the bed that is impossible to reach when putting on new sheets.

LINTHLYPTUS
(lin tu lip' tus)

n. Any cough drop found in one's pocket after a long period of time.

LITMUSLOAD
(lit' mus lode)

n. Any washload that comes out the color of the one item that faded.

MAGLERK
(mag' lurk)

n. Ingenious wedge made in a coffee lid to facilitate safe consumption while driving.

MALTIGO
(mahl' tih go)

n. Temporary state of confusion upon exiting a store in a mall and not remembering which direction one entered by.

MANUMULCHING
(man' yew mul ching)

v. Transporting leaves by sandwiching them between one hand and the rake.

MARGRANE
(mar' grayn)

n. The blinding pain from drinking Margarita slush too quickly.

MAYTAG MASSAGE
(may' tag muh sahj')

n. The momentary thrill experienced while sitting on a washer as it launches into the spin cycle.

McNERTIA
(mak nur' sha)

n. Malaise that prevents a McDonald's employee from filling your order too quickly, or correctly.

MEDIPEEP
(meh' dee peep)

n. Uncontrollable urge to look inside a host's bathroom cabinet to see what kind of afflictions he suffers from.

MEGANEGABAR
(meg uh neg' uh bar)

n. The line you draw across the "amount" section of a check to prevent people from adding, "and a million dollars."

MEMOMIMICRY
(mem oh mim' ih kree)

n. The brief lapse in a phone conversation where you pretend to be getting a pencil to write down an important message.

MEMOSPHERE
(meh' moh sfeer)

n. The part of the sky one searches when trying to recall something in the past.

MINIBLURB
(mih' nee blerb)

n. That useless piece of information about the author found on the back of a book.

MINNIE PEARL VISION
(mih' nee perl' vizh' un)

n. Trying to envision how a pair of drugstore sunglasses will look on you without the huge tag hanging from them.

MINUTATER
(min'u tay tur)

n. The smallest french fry in the bag. (See also **POTENTATER**, the largest french fry in the bag.)

MIRRORCIDE
(mi' rawr side)

n. Leading cause of death among finches and parakeets.

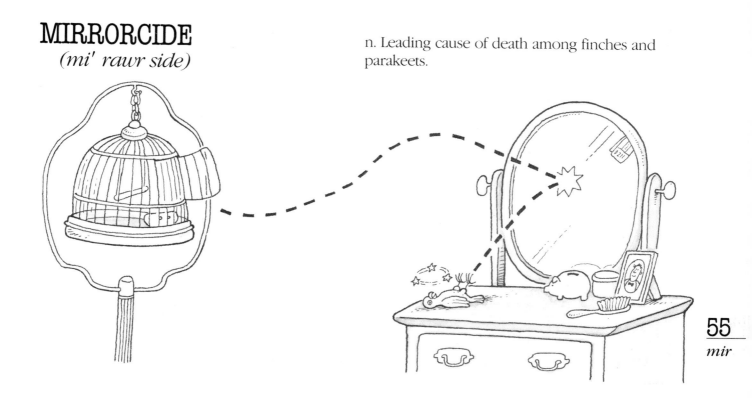

MISSPITS
(mis' spitz)

n. Albino watermelon seeds.

MOLOTOV CARTAIL
(mah' lah tav kar' tayl)

n. Any service station towel used in place of a gas cap.

MOMMENOIA
(mom muh noy' ah)

n. Fear that the dentist or doctor will barge in and catch you playing with his equipment.

MUGPUDDLES
(mug' pud ulz)

n. Small bodies of water that collect on upturned mugs in the dishwasher.

NICAMEASLES
(nik' a mee zulz)

n. Brown dots on the front of a ballplayer's uniform from spitting tobacco and missing.

NINKER
(nin' kur)

n. Any utensil that positions itself inside a drawer to prevent the drawer from opening.

NITVWIT
(nit' vwit)

n. Any person who can't find reverse gear in a Volkswagen.

NOUGALICITY
(noo ga lis' ih tee)

n. Degree to which a Snickers bar will stretch before the caramel snaps.

NOZZLOP
(noz' zlop)

n. To look into a garden hose to see if the water is coming.

NUTRASECOND
(new' truh sek und)

n. The few seconds of pleasure before the after-taste of a diet drink sets in.

NUTTONBUTTON
(nut'n' but'n)

n. The device at intersections marked, "push to cross."

ORQO
(oar' ko)

n. The small bar that turns an "O" into a "Q." (Not to be confused with the Arqo which is the bar that turns an "R" into a drugstore.)

PARSLEYVANIA
(par slee vay' nyuh)

n. The place where all the fancy restaurant garnish that is never eaten comes from.

PASTAPLEGIC
(pas tuh plee' jik)

n. Person who's eaten so much spaghetti he can't move.

PAYFALL
(pay' fal)

n. The phone booth sound that tricks you into thinking your coin accidentally returned.

PEAMORPHO
(pee mor' foh)

n. The peanut butter that escapes through the holes to the other side of the cracker.

PEEPOLA
(pee poe' luh)

n. The gap in the dressing room curtain that can never be completely closed.

PENCICOPTER
(pen' sih kop tur)

n. Classroom invention fashioned from a pencil and a ruler during periods of extreme boredom.

PEPSILLUVIUM
(pep sil lew' vee yum)

n. The tiny amount of cola that escapes when you push a straw through the lid of a soft drink.

PERCALEVATE
(pur kayl' eh vate)

v. To levitate oneself while trying to straighten out the sheets underneath.

PLACEBASE
(pla see' bays)

n. Any item used as a base in a baseball game during an equipment shortage, such as a rock or large turtle.

POPTROOPERS
(pahp' trew purz)

n. Kernels that leap over the side of the container onto the counter when popcorn is being purchased.

POTENTATER
(poh' ten tay tur)

n. The largest french fry in the bag. (See also **MINUTATER**, the smallest french fry in the bag.)

PREMALOOMA
(prem a loo' ma)

n. Any piece of aluminum foil that comes off the roll looking like the state of Nevada.

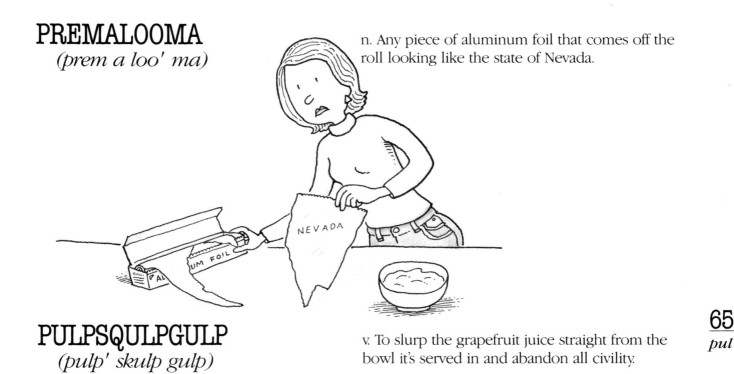

PULPSQULPGULP
(pulp' skulp gulp)

v. To slurp the grapefruit juice straight from the bowl it's served in and abandon all civility.

PURCILIOUS
(per sil' ee us)

adj. The manner in which a man holds his wife's pocketbook in public, as if it contained some odious matter.

FITTING ROOMS

PYRAMONSTER
(pie' ruh mon stur)

n. That thing with one big eye on the back of a dollar bill.

QUADRIPHOBIA
(kwa dri foh' bee yuh)

n. Fear of approaching a four-way stop sign and not knowing "who goes next."

RECOGILOG
(re kog' ih log)

n. The list inside of a library book that you always check to see if you recognize anyone else who wasted time reading it.

REMOTANT
(ree moh' tant)

n. Any alien creature who suddenly appears in the background of a news or feature report.

RETINUS PIGMENTOASTUS
(reh' tih nus pig men tos' tus)

n. Condition of being misled by the tinted window on a toaster oven into thinking something is "done."

REYULERATE
(re yew' lur ayt)

v. To reposition Christmas tree lights so no two of the same colors are beside each other.

RINGS OF RATH AND KAHN
(ringz' uhv rath' and cahn')

n. The mysterious red rings encircling sliced baloney.

ROGERLAND
(rah' jer land)

n. The netherworld from which highway patrolmen suddenly materialize.

ROTOCORONETIC
(roh toh cah roh net' ik)

n. A person who eats corn on the cob in an up and down or "column" style. (See also **SMITHCORONETIC**.)

RUMPHUMP
(rump' hump)

n. The seat on the school bus directly over the rear wheel.

SCHLITZSTOP
(schlits' stop)

n. The one player in amateur softball games who always thinks he can handle his position and a beer at the same time.

SCORBAGE
(skor' bahj)

n. Wadded up trash hurled toward the wastebasket from across the room.

SCOTCHROTOR
(skoch' roh tur)

n. The wheel left behind when all the cellophane tape is used up.

SECOND OILPINION [TO GET A]
(seh'cund oyl pin' yun)

v. Checking a dipstick, wiping it off, then *rechecking* because you never "trust" it the first time.

73
sec

SHOWERSHROUD
(show' ur shrowd)

n. Those hotel shower curtains that inexplicably wrap themselves around you while you shower.

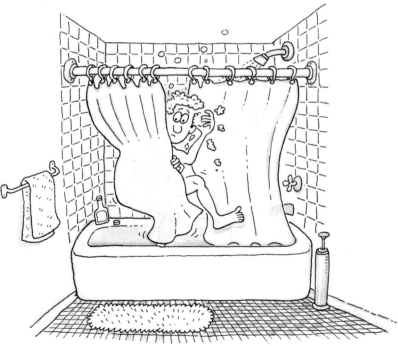

SIZZLAGE
(siz' lidge)

n. The amount of skin one is willing to sacrifice while testing an iron to make sure it won't burn one's shirt.

SKIVLINES
(skiv' lynz)

n. The red or blue lines around jockey shorts that make them resemble fine China.

SLOANTIME
(slown' tym)

n. The difference between real time and the time displayed atop the bank.

SLOOVERS
(sloo' vurz)

n. Remnants of soap too small to use, but too big to throw away.

SLOVERTURE
(slow' vur chur)

n. The distorted music which begins every educational movie.

SMITHCORONETIC
(smith cah roh net' ik)

n. A person who eats corn on the cob in a left to right or "typewriter" style. (See also **ROTOCORONETIC**.)

SMOKEYPOKEY
(smoh kee poh' kee)

n. Inertia that overcomes cars when they suddenly encounter a highway patrolman.

SMOOK
(smewk)

n. The flimsy paper stretched across the examining table at a doctor's office.

SMUGSTICKER
(smug' stih kur)

n. The price tag that normally intelligent people leave on their new car window for months.

SNABBLE
(sna' bul)

v. To attempt to use a sniglet while playing Scrabble.

SPUMPSPEED
(spump' speed)

n. The velocity achieved between speed bumps before having to slow down again.

SQUINCHOOING
(skwin chew' ing)

v. Staring up at the sun to expedite a sneeze.

STOPTIONAL
(stop' shun ul)

n. Any stop sign in the middle of nowhere that no one pays attention to.

SUBWAY SURFERS
(sub' way sur' furz)

n. People on public transportation with the uncanny ability to maintain perfect balance without using the straps.

SUDSORIAN CALENDAR
(sudz oar' ee an ka' len dur)

n. Calendar used on soap operas which allows one day's events to be stretched over a three-week period.

SUZMOSIS
(suz moh' sis)

n. Mysterious disappearance of dishwater even when the sink is stopped airtight.

SWURLEE
(swer' lee)

n. A playground swing wrapped impossibly out of reach.

T-RATION
(tee' ra shun)

v. To use less and less toilet paper as one nears the end of the roll.

TACANGLE
(tak' ang ul)

n. The position of one's head while biting into a taco.

TATERCRATER
(tay' tur kray' tur)

n. Hole dug in mashed potatoes to keep the gravy in.

TELEVELOCITY
(teh leh veh la' sih tee)

n. The speed at which one tries to reach the phone before the answering machine comes on.

BRRRRING

TERMA HELPER
(ter' ma hel' pur)

n. The extra verbiage one uses to stretch a 600-word essay to the required 1000.

TEXAS SEE-SAW MASSACRE
(teks' us see' saw mas' uh kur)

n. When the other person bails off a teeter-totter slamming you to the ground.

THREEK
(threek)

n. A fork with a bent tine.

THRUB
(thrub)

n. The small web of skin between the thumb and index finger that makes us 0.0005% amphibian.

TOASTIPHOBIA
(toh stihfoh' bee yuh)

n. Fear of putting a fork in the toaster even when it is unplugged because, somehow, the toaster "remembers."

TODLITTER
(tod' lit ur)

n. Food debris under a high chair following an attempted feeding.

TRUFITTI
(truh fee' tee)

n. Washing instructions found on the backs of dirty trucks.

TUBLOIDS
(tuhb' loydz)

n. Any periodical reserved for bathroom readings.

TUPPERWARP
(tuh' pur warp)

n. Condition of Tupperware left in the microwave too long.

UHFLAW
(yu' flaw)

n. The one television tuned to a different channel in the bank of televisions at the appliance store.

ULTIMATO
(ul tih may' toe)

n. The choice of eating your vegetables or going to bed without supper.

UMBROGLIO
(um brol' yoh)

n. Any conflict with an umbrella on a windy day.

URMOMMERIZE
(yer mom' mer eyes)

v. To attempt to decipher *exactly* what an upset coach is mouthing on T.V.

VACUBEAM
(vak' yew beem)

n. The useless headlight on a vacuum cleaner.

VEGEMAT
(vej' mat)

n. The green (or brown) leaf of lettuce that supports a lump of jello or cottage cheese.

WALDUST
(wal' dust)

n. Powder that sticks to you when you lean against a white wooden house.

WASHINGTON, ABRAHAM
(wash' ing tun, ay' bra ham)

n. The unidentifiable President on the facsimile bill on a change machine.

WAVOIDS
(way' voydz)

n. People who bob up and down in the ocean trying to stay dry above the waist.

WESEENEMS
(we see' numz)

n. Recreational vehicles plastered with state national parks and American flag decals.

WHATLET
(hwot' let)

n. Any electrical plate on the wall with no holes, and consequently, no purpose whatsoever.

WOB
(wahb)

n. The long weary walk up the aisle at the end of a movie.

YAFFLING
(yah' fling)

v. Speaking loudly to foreigners as if, somehow, this makes you easier to understand.

YEARAGOSTATS
(yeer' uh goh stats)

n. The part of a forecast that tells you what the weather was like a year ago so you'll feel even more miserable.

YUMP
(yump)

v. To punch one's glove in anticipation of an arriving baseball.

ZEBBITS
(zeb' itz)

n. Those bizarre fireplace tools whose function no one seems able to explain.

ZIPPIJIG
(zih' pih jig)

n. The dance one performs whenever a rubber band is pointed at them.

OFFICIAL SNIGLETS ENTRY BLANK

Dear Rich:

I've searched through every dictionary known to man and cannot find the following word. Why?

_____

_____

_____

_____

_____

Sincerely,

m(name) _____

(street address) _____

(city, state, zip code) _____

SNIGLETS
P.O. Box 2350
Hollywood, CA 90078